Mixed Media
Storytelling
Workbook

Art Journaling Inspiration, Words and Prompts

Edited by Kristy Conlin

NORTH LIGHT BOOKS
Cincinnati, Ohio
createmixedmedia.com

Contents

What You'll Need 3

Introduction 5

1
Yes, You Can Do This! 6

2
Text Design 24

3
What to Write 52

4
Visual Journaling 104

Resources 122

About the Authors 124

Index 126

Tape
from *Wide Open* by Randi Feuerhelm-Watts

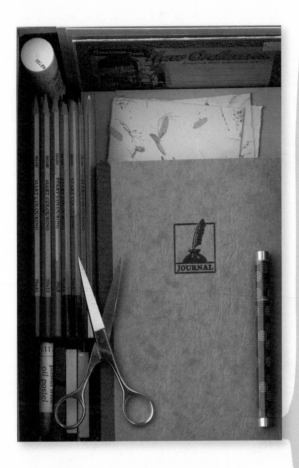

What You'll Need

Here is a complete list of supplies mentioned in the techniques and projects in this book. You don't have to use all of them and in many cases you may decide you like one product better than another.

For more mixed-media storytelling inspiration scan the QR code with your smartphone or visit createmixedmedia.com/mixed-media-storytelling.

1 " (2.5cm) foam brush

6B pencil

acrylic paint

blue ink

box

bulletin board

colored pencils

crayons (not water-soluble)

dimensional fabric paint

duct tape

electrical tape

ephemera (tags, bits of paper, stickers, etc.)

gel medium

gel pen

gesso

glue

graphite pencils

highlighter

ink

journal

large sheet of drawing or crafting paper

liquid acrylics

loose paper

magazine, newspaper or book pages

markers

markers with brush and chisel tips

masking tape

metallic markers

paint pen

Paintastick Brush Pen and Magic Wand (Elmer's)

paintbrushes

palettes

pens

permanent markers

poster marker

printed text

pushpins

Red Wide marker

rubber stamps

scissors

stencils

water recepticle

water-soluble crayons

watercolor paint

watercolor pencils

whiteout pens

writing notebook or other paper for collage separate from journal

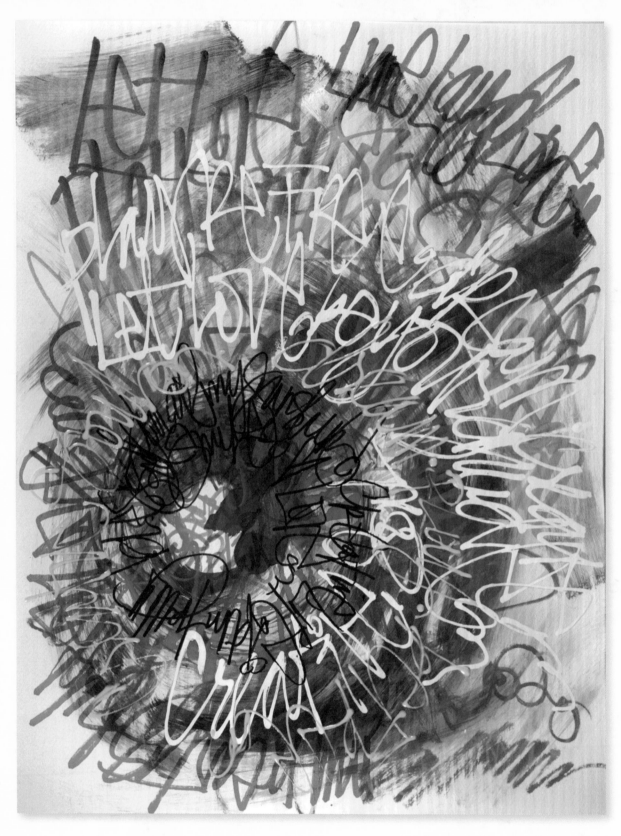

Continuous Writing
from *Doodles Unleashed* by Traci Bautista

Introduction

Pssst. Hey, you—

Have a story to tell?

Want to scream it from the mountain top?

Or maybe you're the hold-it-close-to-your-heart type.

Want to create a document to share with those who come after you?

Or perhaps you have in mind something for your eyes only, something to reflect upon in solitude.

Either way—any way—this is the book—the journal—for you.

Because this isn't like other art books.

This is your book.

We're just here to help you write it . . .

to put down words . . .

to find your voice and your confidence . . .

to embellish.

We intend for the two of you to form a close relationship, this book and you. We've included a lot of blank pages to go along with all the absolutely amazing prompts and ideas provided by some of the most popular and inspiring authors and artists we've had the pleasure to work with. With authors like Quinn McDonald guiding you, you'll be inspired to write. How could you not be? Use her "Box of Words" idea for new inspiration every day. Liz Lamoreux and the Journal Fodder Junkies both share easy (and, we promise, FUN!) lessons for writing poetry and making it a staple of your journal. And Randi Feuerhelm-Watts finds inspiration in today's headlines as well as in lists of all kinds. We think you will, too!

But we know that sometimes the hardest part is getting started. Hey, we've all been there. That nagging voice that says we aren't good enough? The one that says no one wants to hear what we have to say? This book is *so* going to help you over that hurdle. You will look what we call your gremlin right in the eye and send him packing with any of several techniques offered here. Not only will your inner critic be quieted, you might just end up learning a thing or two about just how strong you are. Oh, and you might just create some pretty cool art, too. Bonus!

Finally, while the words you write will likely be the BIG STARS here, we think they should feel special. So you'll find tutorials on fanciful lettering, writing in paths and more. Maybe you're not quite ready for the world to read your innermost thoughts. With artful continuous writing and bold paint-spilling techniques you'll learn how to keep private what you want to keep private.

It's true, you know: We all have a story to tell. Isn't it time you told yours?

— Kristy Conlin and the North Light Books team

P.S. Surely you don't need to be reminded . . . but this is *your* book. And ultimately, it might not be the most practical journal with all these other pages in it, preprinted as they are. So in addition to owning it, might we suggest that you *own* it? When you are done reading this page, gesso over it and then write on top of it. Or rip it out and make an envelope out if it and adhere the envelope to page 83 and hide a secret in it. Or cut it up and use the words for found poetry or to inspire a journal entry or story. Or rip it out and throw it in the garbage. Paint the cover. Or collage over it. Maybe distress it.

This is, after all, your story. It should look like it.

Yes, You Can Do This!

Dealing with the Gremlin
From *Raw Art Journaling* by Quinn McDonald

So, what gets in the way of play? Your own negative self-talk—the defeating, horrible things you say to yourself that deflate your ego and squelch any talent you may have. Does any of this sound like what you say to yourself?

"You're no good at this, why even try?"
"You call this art? Who would buy this mess?"
"You're not really an artist, you never will be."

This negative self-talk is a gremlin that chews through your self-confidence and self-esteem. The gremlin is not ready for your creative growth; it is ready for lack and attack, so it always points to how you will fail, starve and turn into a bag lady, even if you are a man. The gremlin is always ready to challenge play and turn wonder into gnawing self-doubt. Everyone has a gremlin, but artists have big, powerful gremlins because for years they have been told that creative work is not "real" work. Creative work is suspect because it might be fun, and certainly, if we have fun, we will do nothing important. Creative work is the reason we are on earth. Creative work connects us all.

Your gremlin is a part of you, and you cannot get rid of it, because it lives in your brain, but you can distance yourself from the negative self-talk. You can, with practice, tell the gremlin to shut up, and do it successfully.

How do you quiet the gremlin? You confront, you confine, you confound.

Confront
Recognize the gremlin's voice so you can separate it from your creative work. Become familiar with the most common phrases you hear in your head. Create a mental image of your gremlin. It is easier to distance yourself from the lack-and-attack messages if you create a picture of your gremlin as a nonhuman figure—something like a monster. Use your imagination to create a visual of all the things the gremlin represents. Make it ugly and mean—and not you. Distance yourself from its negative influence.

Write a description or draw your gremlin on a sheet of paper—not on a page in your journal. (Once a gremlin is in your journal, you'll keep running across him. Use a separate piece of paper.)

My gremlin is a series of triangles—sharp points that he uses to poke and bother me.

Now divide the paper in half. On the left side, write what the gremlin says most often. On the right side, write a response to each comment in positive terms. If your gremlin says, "You're not an artist," write that on the left side. On the right, you might answer, "I create fine art; any art I create is fine with me!" (Thanks to Lynn Trochelman for sending me that wonderful piece of wisdom!) Keep writing till you feel better. You can do this exercise as often as you like. It works over and over again.

You can also draw an image of your gremlin and have speech balloons coming out of his mouth. Spend some time creating the gremlin. If you can't draw, that's fine. You can just use lines and shapes to represent negative energy.

Confine

When you draw and write about your gremlin on a separate sheet of paper, you can control what happens to it. Put it face down in a drawer when you begin your creative work. Fold up the paper and sit on it while you are in your studio. Crumple it up and throw it into a corner or out of the room. Separating yourself from your gremlin is powerful. The image of throwing the beast away from you, or putting the paper in a place where you can't see it while you work, gives you real power. Always distance yourself from the negative self-talk when you're in the studio.

Confound

You are intimately familiar with your negative self-talk. You probably play it as background noise in your head. When you take charge of your creative work, you befuddle the gremlin—reduce its power and hold over you. That's exactly what you want. For this reason, don't destroy the paper. Negative self-talk has been a part of your life for a long time, and you need to keep finding new ways to distance yourself from your gremlin. Physically being able to displace the gremlin as it lives on the paper allows you to do this most easily. Confounding him over and over again clears your head.

What the Gremlin Says / Rephrased as Encouragement

What the Gremlin Says	Rephrased as Encouragement
"You aren't an artist."	I create fine art; any art I create is fine with me!
"You'll never be able to sell this."	I'm going to satisfy myself first, then decide what to do next.
"Who cares about art, anyway?"	I make time for creative projects because they're important to me.

Distancing Yourself From Your Gremlin

Draw him on a sheet of paper separate from your journal. You are in control of the piece of paper. Hang it on your bulletin board to remind yourself to answer the negative self-talk with positive statements.

- Use the piece of paper to confine the gremlin. Every time you start creative work, talk to the gremlin as you put it out of the studio or face down in a drawer. Limiting the time the gremlin can talk to you limits your own negative self-talk.

- Create a ritual of taking the gremlin out of your studio while you work. Make it part of how you start your creative time. Find funny places to put the gremlin—under the doormat, in the linen closet, under the spare toilet paper rolls—to remind yourself that he has no power over you.

- Draw your gremlin to suit your mood. Some days he might be ugly and mean, some days he'll be all eyes—the better to criticize your work—some days he'll have a tail and horns. If you don't want to make him a monster or reptile, you can use lines and shapes to create tension. You'll get better at this over time.

- Even when you are not in your studio, watch out for negative self-talk. Replace it with something positive that is true. If you are scared to talk to people about your art, instead of using "I'm not scared," say, "I'll understand my art better if I explain it to others," as a positive replacement.

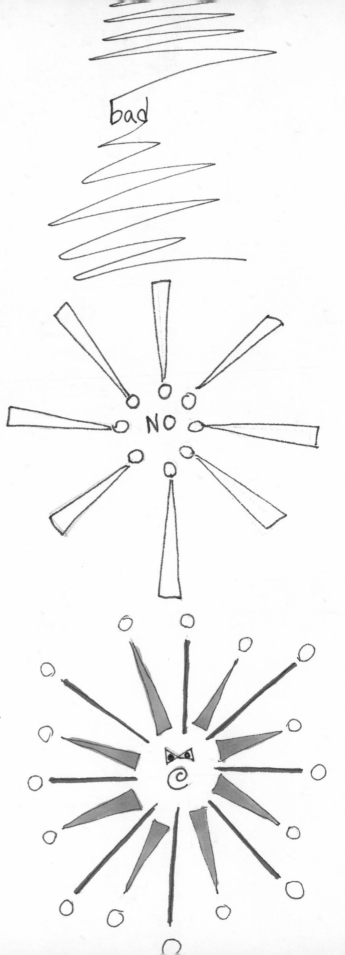

What does your gremlin or inner critic look like? What color is it? If it had a name what would it be? Draw your gremlin on a loose piece of paper, then attach it facedown here. Draw something positive on top to reduce the gremlin's negative power.

Maybe you have more than one gremlin. Or maybe he's throwing a party and bringing his friends—gremlins playing poker, anyone? It's time to exorcise them, too!

If you could dismiss your gremlin in any way possible, how would you? A one-way ticket to Siberia? Send him to the bottom of the ocean to swim with the fishies? Send him out into a beautiful field full of wildflowers to feel the sun on his face and melt that bitter stone of a heart? Write and/or draw your gremlin-demolishing fantasy here!

Do you know that critical inner voice that tells you you're not good enough or not talented enough, or that warns you not to take risks? I always think of my inner critic in the fitting term coined by noted counselor and personal and executive coach Richard Carson: the gremlin (in fact, he wrote a book called *Taming Your Gremlin* and is founder of the Gremlin Taming Institute). Regardless of what you call this voice, everyone has one.

Art journaling is a good way to silence your inner critic. Rather than ignoring him when you begin your art journal (which can be easier said than done!), try giving him a voice on a journal page. It can be a visual voice, a literal voice or both. If you can have a dialogue with this critic and actually imagine him outside of yourself, then you can separate that voice from your own. You will begin to see that what the critic says to you is no longer relevant.

What does your inner voice look like? Is it male or female? What color is it? If it had a name what would it be? Draw your inner critic and include a dialogue with him on the page. Then, when he has had his say, turn to a clean page and get ready to begin!

HOW do You EAT AN elePHANt?

— ouch!

ONe Bite at a time! Take art making 1 step at a time. Begin with practising doodling, making faces, drawing from nature, make BoRDers, create Backgrounds Practise drawing florishes then put it all together! There... now wasn't that easier than you thought?

I'm over-whelmed
just take one step at a time
But I'm not talented
oh yes you are... you just have to find your
groove
You can do it!
how do I find my Style?
By trying different styles & combining them...
yours will emerge!
How can I get better?
By lots of practise and not being afraid of making mistakes

What does your gremlin or inner critic say? What can you say to refute your gremlin's negative talk? What color is it? If it had a name what would it be? Draw your inner critic and include a dialogue with him on the page.

Taming the Critic: Self-Portrait

From *Journal Spilling* by Diana Trout

Inner critics are tricky little buggers. They sneak up on us at the most inopportune time—sometimes we don't even know they're there. Here are some clues that your critic is present:

- You feel that your idea is silly, stupid, not worth the price of materials or time, and you feel that you are not an "artist" or a "writer" anyway.
- You feel overwhelmed by a project.
- You are rolling along with a project, doing whatever comes next. Suddenly you stop and say, "Well . . . I was thinking I should do such-and-such next, but maybe I should wait."

Say "hello critic" if any of these scenarios rings true.

Working with your critic is an ongoing process. I was surprised to discover my little devil whispering in my ear when I started working on this section of the book you are holding. Rats!

One good way of learning to identify your critic is to get to know him or her through the writing and drawing process. Once you've gotten to know your critic a little better, you may want to take the next step.

You may need to fire your critic or, at the least, demote her. You'll do whatever works for you. Take your time; revisit the topic often. I could devote an entire journal to my critic.

Come along for the ride with an open mind.

Self-Portrait

For this project, you can easily break the steps into manageable time bites. Do the writing in one sitting; come back later and try the watercolor. While that is drying, do the self-portrait. Cut the portrait out and glue it in if the watercolor pages are dry and you have time. Come back to finish it when you have 45 minutes to an hour.

Materials list

- journal
- water-soluble crayons (Caran d'Ache or Portfolio)
- 6B pencil
- scissors
- gel medium
- gesso (white)
- glue
- writing notebook or other lightweight paper for collage

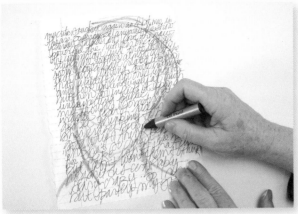

1 Begin with a spill-written page using the prompt, My Critic. Working quickly, loosely sketch a self-portrait using a water-soluble crayon for its gooshy smooshy line or a soft lead pencil, if you prefer. I hear you say, "Aack! What?! Draw a self-portrait?!" OK, calm down.

You need to draw an oval, held up by a column, resting on top of a couple of foothills—easy enough, right? Practice this a couple of times. Try using your whole arm to draw, not just your hand. Get your arm moving and draw around the shape until you are happy with it. The art police will not arrest you for making a "bad" self-portrait. It doesn't even need to look like you. It could be a creature, a dog, a cat, a bird, a house—whatever you want. Loosely interpret the word "self-portrait."

2 Cut out your portrait shape—loosely. I had sketched out a few, so I cut each of them out. It's nice to have a few choices and then have leftovers for another page.

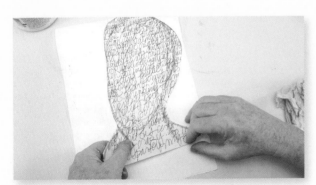

3 Use gel medium to glue the portrait down to a gessoed page in your journal. Go with your gut feeling when gluing your portrait to the page. I glued mine in the middle of the left-hand page on my spread. As it turned out, I wrote around my self-portrait, and it looked like I was in a cloud of words. You may want to place yours higher on the page, as if you are looking down on the swirl of words, or perhaps lower as if you are being buried under the words.

4 Watercolor spill around the image. I try not to plan these spills at all. I simply reach for the first color I see. It is so often red! I never, ever wear red and, outside of my journal, rarely reach for it first. Sounds like I need to do a journal page about that, right? You can add Caran d'Ache to this watercolor layer as well. Just be sure to water it into the page so that you can write over it.

5 Thin some gesso with a couple of drops of water and apply it on top of the watercolor. I wanted to obscure the writing in the background a little bit. You could scribble into the gesso layer using a pencil or the non-business end of a brush. Add patterns, words, borders or small drawings. Allow this to dry.

6 Begin writing again, asking yourself questions about your critic. I used a water-soluble crayon. You could use a pencil for this step.

7 Add some color and small details to your portrait. (Don't panic; details may be loose as well.) I wanted red hair (even though my hair is gray and brown). I gave myself a beaky bird nose too. Your portrait does not have to look like you! I used a water-soluble crayon to outline my eyes and nose; you may want to use a pencil.

8 Maybe you'd like to add some shapes to your background? I decided to add linked circles using a water-soluble crayon. Perhaps I'd write in them or collage? No need to have a plan here. If you think you might want to write inside your shapes, try gluing circles of paper in their centers. I added thin rice paper over three of the circles. Again, no real plan needed.

9 Ah! How about turning to a random page in the dictionary? Close your eyes and pick a word.

Glue the word where your instincts tell you—don't think about it. I glued my word on top of one of the rice paper circles.

Things that happen when you work intuitively are always so much more interesting. Give it a try and be patient and open-minded.

Identify Your Critic

I wanted to get a visual on my critic so that I could recognize him. In order to do that, I asked myself (and answered) the following questions. You might find it helpful to ask yourself these same questions about your own critic.

- Is my critic male or female? (male)
- Does my critic remind me of anyone in my real life? (oh, yeah)
- What are my critic's favorite foods? (liver and onions)
- Where does my critic go on vacation? (The Wax Museum)
- What is your critic's favorite book? (calculus textbooks)
- What does your critic wear? (black pants, shoes and tie; white shirt and socks)
- What is your critic's favorite expression? ("Tsk, tsk, tsk.")
- What is your critic's favorite breakfast food? (black coffee, Wheaties)
- How many pillows are on your critic's bed? (one very flat pillow)
- What color is his/her kitchen? (white)
- Does he/she have any hobbies? (balancing his checkbook)

You get the idea. Go ahead and write down a bunch of questions. They could even be multiple choice such as:

Where does my critic live?
  a) Rural area
  b) Suburbia
  c) In an apartment just off the Jersey Turnpike so he can easily get to work in the morning

What is your critic's favorite color?
  a) Hot pink
  b) Turquoise
  c) Gray

What is your critic's favorite sight?
  a) Daffodils in a spring breeze
  b) Flocks of birds swooping around in the sky
  c) His computer, searching for the solution to some algebraic equation

It took me a while for my critic's name to reveal itself to me. I woke up one morning thinking Stewie. His name is Stewie. You may decide to apply a name to your critic more quickly. I waited until it occurred to me.

Notes for identifying your inner critic:

Is my critic male or female?

Does my critic remind me of anyone in my real life?

What are my critic's favorite foods?

Where does my critic go on vacation?

What is my critic's favorite book?

What does my critic wear?

What is my critic's favorite expression?

What is my critic's favorite breakfast food?

How many pillows are on my critic's bed?

What color is his/her kitchen?

Does he/she have any hobbies?

Where does my critic live?

What is my critic's favorite color?

What is my critic's favorite sight?

Anything else:

This might be a great page upon which to place your self-portrait.

2

Text

Experimenting With Text and Tools

From *The Journal Junkies Workshop* by Eric M. Scott and David R. Modler

It is easy to get in the habit of writing in the visual journal using the same handwriting forms all the time. It becomes hard to break comfortable, lazy text styles. There are many quick and simple ways to shake up your writing. Here are some of the options.

Stencils
Plastic stencils come in a variety of fonts and sizes, and you can use them with pencils, markers, paints and other media. Keep thin stencils in a pocket in the journal so they are handy and accessible. You can even create your own stencils from posterboard or flexible plastic sheets in order to have unique and personal lettering on hand at any given moment.

Stamps
You can also use rubber stamps with a variety of media from traditional stamp ink to paint. Just clean the stamps thoroughly after use to avoid damaging them. You can even carve your own stamps from old corks or rubber erasers for unique and personal lettering. Remember to reverse the letter when you carve it so it stamps in the correct orientation.

Drawn Text
Draw large and dynamic letters and words into your journal. Such letters and words act as graphic devices—elements that rely on visual impact. Block and bubble letters are examples of letters that take on a graphic nature. Experiment with size, style and color as you hand draw text and words.

Printed Text
Thanks to the convenience of computers and the Internet, printed text is now a common element used for embellishment. You can quickly print and glue words, quotes and other text into your journal. Your text can be relevant to the content of a page or random and oddly juxtaposed. Printed text can even be transferred using image transfer techniques.

Found Text
Everything from telephone book pages to newspapers to flyers and copies can be glued into the journal. It is not necessary that the text relate to the theme or the idea of the page. It is enough that it gives the page texture and layers.

Quotes, Poems and Lyrics

Meaningful quotes, poems and song lyrics are yet another source of text for your journal. The words can be printed, handwritten, drawn or transferred. Often lyrics of the songs you listen to while journaling make their way onto the page as they get into your head.

Note Taking

Because the visual journal can travel with you, it is a natural place to take notes, whether as a student in a class or as a worker in a business meeting. Because of the visual nature of the journal, visual learners may even remember the notes better. If you write notes in your journal, you can still highlight key concepts and important information.

Altered Books

Some people prefer to journal in an old book and will glue together pages to create thick, durable foundations. The book's preexisting text can be hidden, obscured or incorporated into the page. Using an altered book takes away the blank, white page, and adds an instant first layer. It is fine to ignore the text that is there and journal right on top of it.

Another way to shake up your writing is to experiment with the type of writing implement you use.

Try a variety of writing and drawing materials. In the examples below, water has been brushed over the water-soluble materials to give you an idea of how you can further manipulate your writing.

Materials list

graphite pencils

pens

colored pencils

watercolor pencils

markers

watercolor crayons

regular crayons

A variety of graphite pencils

A variety of pens

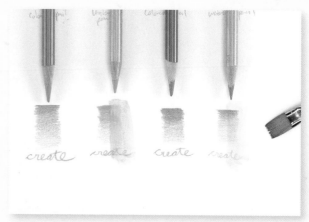

Regular and watercolor pencils

A variety of markers

Regular and watercolor crayons

The next several pages are reserved for play and experimentation. Play with stencils and stamps—try creating your own. Draw text and fill it in with a variety of different implements.

Ooh, song lyrics are a great idea for this kind of thing. Try writing a line from a favorite song and using it as a prompt.

Maybe there's a song that easily comes to mind that you just. can't. stand. That could make an even better, more challenging and more interesting prompt.

Maybe you'd like to use these pages to create swatches. Test out your pencils, pens, markers and crayons here and use the results for future reference.

Doodle Warm-Up

From *Collage Unleashed* by Traci Bautista

Doodling doesn't have to be limited to board meetings and phone calls. This exercise will instantly boost your creative metabolism and free up your spirit of play. Remember, there are no rules. You can even close your eyes, if you like.

Materials list

large sheet of drawing or crafting paper

colored pencils

assortment of black and colored markers

gel pens

whiteout pen

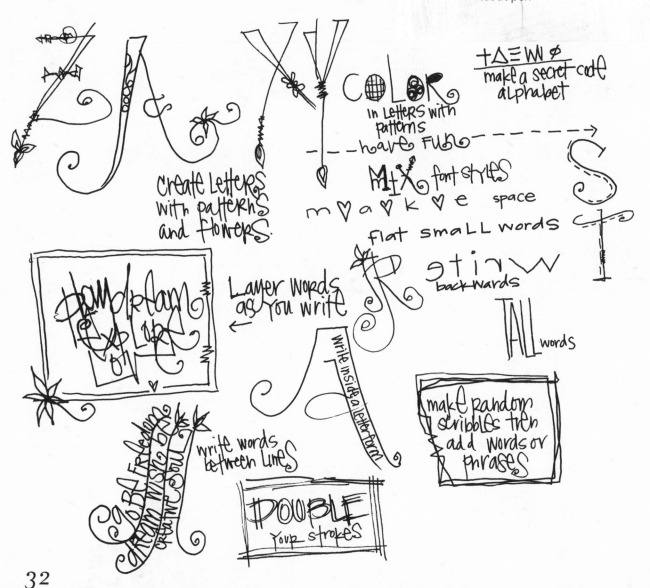

Fill a Page

Take a large sheet of drawing paper or craft paper and complete the following tasks: Write the alphabet (large), over the entire piece of paper, using colored pencils or markers. Next, write words that describe your day over the top of the alphabet. Continue to fill your paper with doodles and patterns, such as geometric shapes, floral patterns—whatever strikes you—using gel pens, markers, a whiteout pen and alternating colors. Experiment with writing letters short and tall, wide or with a swirl. Write randomly over the page. Don't think about placement, just work fast and let the words and marks flow!

Use the finished piece as it is, in collage work or make copies of it to use in future projects.

There's a large sheet of paper right here. Why not try a stylized alphabet? Maybe frilly, curlicue letters are your style. Or maybe something more industrial-inspired. Either way, pencils, markers, colored pencils and pens would all be appropriate for this exercise.

Maybe on this page you'd like to try Traci Bautista's "Fill a Page" exercise. You know you want to! Write randomly over the page. Don't think about placement, just work fast, and let the words tumble onto the page. Then fill in the gaps with doodles. Now sit back and admire your work. Or plan how you might use this work in another project.

Fanciful Lettering

From *Journal Bliss* by Violette

From the exquisite markings of the ancient Sanskrit writings to modern-day text, humans have always been fascinated by the art of making marks to communicate their thoughts and ideas. Incorporating lettering as part of our artwork is a natural extension of this and an important part of visual journaling.

When I was a teenager I bought a Speedball lettering book, some ink pens and nibs and began trying to imitate proper, perfect letter forms. Try as I might, I was unsuccessful. Number one, I don't like following rules, and number two, I'm not much of a perfectionist (in fact, I've abolished that word from my vocabulary!). I sure wish I had had a teacher back then who had encouraged me to develop my own style of lettering and to toss out the rules. Instead, it took me a couple of decades before I gave myself permission to develop my very own fanciful lettering.

Years ago I began drawing and selling cartoons. I amassed a number of cartooning books with instructions on how to letter in a cartoon style, and from them I learned how to fit the letters into one another to make the words appear more personal and finished. But most of all, I learned that creating your own lettering is so much more fun than struggling with formal letter forms.

Developing your own style of lettering is a fun way of personalizing your journal pages and adding a wonderful artsy dimension to your work. That's not to say you can't use computer-generated journaling—or even words and phrases clipped from books and magazines—but if that's your style, try using artistic hand lettering in combination with these methods to add your own *je ne sais quoi* to your work!

The best way to get to the place where you like your own writing is simply to practice. My mom, who is an avid scrapbooker, used to say that she could not use her handwriting in her pages because it was illegible. I encouraged her to practice, and she began using a light box to trace my words (she really likes my swirly lettering). Before you know it, she could handwrite her pages as well as doodle along the borders freehand. If my mom can do it, so can you.

Let's take a look at some ways to create your own lettering and experiment with a variety of tools in order to add your own inimitable imprint to your artwork.

Materials list

- variety of pens, pencils and other writing utensils in a variety of colors
- paint
- paintbrushes

Bliss Joy ABundance

Gratitude Play Explore!

Let Silly in!= Love Laugh

Live Be Joyful ♡ SPRead your Wings

Mix ScRipt and Printing TogetHeR

Just FoR fun! Have fun

Spill OpeN; Allow Let it Be

Don't worry ABout Being Messy.

Life iS Messy & very Real "and juicy"

EmBrace it All...the good and

the so-called Bad ★ hold a space for

WoNdeR to move into...it's Magic

Gee, wouldn't this be a great place to practice even more lettering? That's right, it would be. But it might also be fun to make a collage of cool typography and writing samples to use as inspiration.

Tape

From *Wide Open* by Randi Feuerhelm-Watts

You don't have to be an expert at calligraphy in order to journal. All kinds of variations of text can be used alone or combined to add interesting visual elements—often becoming an important part of the composition.

Do something different. Try using black electrical tape. Tape it across the page and write on it with a white paint pen. Masking tape can be used in the same way, and it comes in different colors and widths. Paint over the top with liquid acrylics; then write directly on top.

Duct tape comes in tons of colors now and works great with permanent pens. You can also wrap it around the edges of each page to add an interesting border. Nontransparent packing tape wraps well, too, and makes the edges of the pages thicker and easier to handle.

Try combining different styles of your own handwriting. Elongate your handwriting simply by stretching it across the page. Try using a paintbrush, painting all in caps with your opposite hand and don't forget a plain old no.2 pencil. Mix different-sized rubber-stamp alphabet sets. Stencils come in all different fonts and sizes, and handheld label makers are a great way to punch out words that come with a sticky backing ready to attach right to the page.

Don't forget the crossword puzzle in the daily paper. Cut it out and glue it down, adding your own words of interest. Cut out titles of articles. Use them just the way they are instead of trying to form your own sentence.

Materials list

- electrical tape
- paint pen
- liquid acrylics
- paintbrush
- duct tape
- masking tape
- rubber stamps
- ink

46

Medical tape works well for this technique also, as does washi tape, which is lightweight and sometimes semitransparent. Plus, washi tape comes in all sorts of fabulous colors and patterns. Metallic, white or contrasting inks will make your tape text a standout.

Don't you just love the idea of working with crossword puzzles and such? Newspaper headlines (from *The News of the World* perhaps? How much fun would that be?) are a unique idea and would result in a very cool graphic black-and-white look. Or paint over your headlines with a light wash of watercolor paint. Ahhh . . . stupendous!

3

What to Write

Daily Journal Writing

From *The Journal Junkies Workshop* by Eric M. Scott and David R. Modler

Many visual journalists use the visual journal like a traditional journal and write in the journal every day or nearly every day. It is easy enough to grab a pen, pencil or marker and write about what has occurred each day. Some people fill pages, and others sum up the day in a few short phrases or a couple of sentences. When combined with paint, collage and other imagery, words create a visual diary. Drawings and bits and pieces of ephemera bring daily life into the journal in a very tangible way.

The visual journal, like a traditional journal, can be a place to vent frustrations, to deal with pains and heartaches or to celebrate life's milestones. The addition of images, color and artistic techniques gives this type of journaling added power, strength and meaning. Memories are quickly sparked at a glance, giving the visual journalist instant recall of a day, a place, a person or an event. Every moment is significant the moment it occurs. The visual journal provides a place to record the nuances of those events before they slip away and are forgotten.

By writing about your life, you begin to create a cherished artifact—something you will want to look over and savor. The visual journal is a true extension of you, and you can pour your life, your thoughts, your hopes and your fears into its pages.

You may be apprehensive about getting personal in the visual journal, fearing that someone may see it and read it. But it is your journal and your journey, and it can be as private or as public as you wish it to be. You can keep a visual journal all for yourself or you can share it with the world—so get as deep, raw and personal as you like.

Materials list

journal

writing instrument of choice

Fifth Grade Team from Wilmington

Go Global
Jakki Gail

Integrated Units
novel-based instruction
community story quilt ★ SOCIAL STUDIES
crop growth simulation ★ SCIENCE
connections ★ MATH
internet ★ TECHNOLOGY
writing ★ WRITING PROMPTS
literature ★ LITERATURE CIRCLES

AR Books to help w/ Character Ed.

Melinda Avis and Mary   Washington
BEAUFORT

WHAT DIFFERENCE
DOES DIFFERENCE MAKE

YOGI E

bauhaus Philosophy

From FRANKLIN
Cecilia
Melisa
Ann

form follows function...
function can also follow form

Building Community is the Foundation

Learning Areas Development
systems in place

CENTERS:
Clay
puppets
reading
sand box
co-op learning

BECOME A CARING COMMUNITY OF ACTIVE LEARNERS

PINEHURST   TUGRAT = SIGNATURE
Sojourn into Learning
ACHIEVE & EXCEL

looked at writing tests
looked for trends
weaknesses
conventions

Giftedness in POVERTY

INCLUSION
all children can learn

• free themselves from negative situations
• hard work and study will pay off
• there is an attitude that gifted students cannot exist in the low-socio-economic community

Yes, this is your journal. Fill it however you desire. Write whatever you wish. Have something on your mind? Something deep? Dark? Secret? Not quite sure you're ready to spill it on these pages? Feel the fear, the anxiety, the excitement, and do it anyway. Then seal it up in an envelope and tape it to the page, or write it in graphite and obscure it by brushing over it with water. Or paint over it with gesso or acrylic paint. The options for hiding your secrets within these pages are limited only by your imagination.

Box of Words

From *Raw Art Journaling* by Quinn McDonald

Words come and go quickly. It's easy to forget that new word you heard this morning. The shortest pencil beats the longest memory, so write down the words you like. To begin your play with words, make each word feel important by writing it down on a tag—you can find tags in office supply stores, or you can make them.

You will need a special place to keep your words. A small box is fine. You can use one you already have—a small but sentimental jewelry box or a hollowed-out altered book work well. Or you might want to make a special box just for this purpose. I keep my tags in an origami box—sometimes called a Masu—that I made.

If you want to make your own origami box, many websites offer directions on the Internet. A 12" (30cm) square will create a perfect starter box.

Materials list

tags or bits of paper

box

writing instrument of choice

No doubt, there are also words you don't like. Not just because of their meaning, but because they sound unfinished, awkward or harsh. Here are some that grate on me: Chunky. Phlegm. Diagonal. You don't have to have a reason, your heart knows. I don't ignore these words, though. They, too, have a place in your collection. They add new color to the words you do like.

When you play with words, it's more interesting to collect and use words that give you a wide range of emotion. You might not like rooms that are dark, unscrupulous people or eating squash, but the words *dark*, *unscrupulous* and *squash* are interesting and may provide welcome contrast with words you do like. If you don't like the sound of a word, try using it with a word you do like to see if it creates a new meaning entirely—one you find exciting. "Dark shiver" sounds mysterious. "Squash petals" can be both an action you take and the petals of a squash plant. Words that combine to create different meanings are too inter-esting to discard. Some words can be both things or actions—*gauge*, *drill*, *ink*, *smile*, *drink*, *tree*.

Avoid words that trigger a strong unpleasant con-notation or emotional connection. You are making meaning, not nightmares.

Should you keep words you like in the same box as the ones you don't like? Try them in separate boxes first. Play with the exercises that follow and see if you want to keep them separated. You can also put them in one box and separate them by using a different color for words you like and those you don't. Or you can use different tag shape—rectangles for the words you like and triangles for the ones you don't. Another option is to put a blue stripe on the tags of words you like and a red stripe on the ones you don't like, or make the tags a different size. You have choices, but you can also dec-orate all the tags just for fun and mix them together. You'll know what to do when the words begin to take on special meaning in your journal.

Here are some words you might like to put in your box:

Shiver
Journey
Petals
Tabulate
Indigo
Bamboo
Glow

Use this page to record all those words you encounter that might make good prompts. Remember to mix it up by including words you don't like or that strike you as humorous. When you are ready to write, you can simply pick a word off this page, or do like Quinn McDonald does and create a box of words.

Stuck? Pick a word, any word. Maybe something flowy and mellifluous, something that appeals to your senses.

Stuck? Pick a word, any word. Maybe something that your brain has a viscerally negative reaction to.

Stuck? Pick a word, any word. Try something that sounds funny to you or that makes you giggle.

Revealing the Poet Within

From *Inner Excavation* by Liz Lamoreux

Writing poetry can seem intimidating, but it can also help us tell our stories in new and unique ways. We all have a bit of poetry inside us; it's just a matter of finding a way to get it onto paper.

How do we do this? By inviting the inner chatter to rest while we investigate, we quiet the mind; we slow down and allow this writing to take on an almost meditative feel. When the negative thoughts appear, we can acknowledge them and then move on. I don't mean to make it sound easy. This is something that can take years of practice. However, just beginning this practice is a powerful tool.

Photography is a tool to help with writing our poetry stories. Photos taken by another person can reveal new layers to us. Note that I don't mean the family photos taken on your most recent vacation. Those invite you to remember how you wish you had lost that extra five pounds before getting on the plane. Rather, I mean someone capturing a photo that invites you to pause and really look at yourself in a new, positive way.

When I dance, I feel very at home in my body. When I came across a photo someone else had taken of me using my camera, I felt moved to write about the freedom I feel when dancing. The photo certainly isn't my favorite photo ever taken of me, yet it conveys the movement of dancing and the joy I experience when I move my body. I was truly lost in the dancing when this joy was captured so I began there when I sat down to write the following:

I see her.

I see her grounded in her body as she moves across the floor, across the room, with arms twirling above her head. And her hips—those hips that shift and turn and twist to the beat of the song in the air. They twist and turn and she moves. How she moves to the music that seems to be part of her. It is as though she is directly connected to the boom ba boom of the beat of the sound in the air. She is directly connected to the soul of the singer and the rhythm as she moves and twists and twirls. Her long hair becomes another extension of the body as her hips circle and her knees bend and her toes point and her arms that once belonged to a ballerina remember what it feels like to stretch, as though they reach for the very moment when she first put on the ballet shoes and smiled that four-year-old girl's smile of joy.

I see her and marvel at how she lets go of the need to wonder what others are thinking or how she must look as her size sixteen body sinks inside the boom ba boom. She lets go of what others are thinking as she stretches her arms to either side and finds the rhythm with her fingertips and wrists as her hips rotate and her knees bend and her feet move quickly with purpose. Her feet move with a purpose that wraps the entire room in a circle that vibrates with joy.

I see her reflection as she twists and stretches and seems grounded in her body.

I see her and I see me.

I see me.

And I dance on.

Giving voice to our bodies is another way to turn our awareness inward and away from focusing on just the physical appearance of our bodies. Imagine what your knees might say as they rest at the end of the day, how your shoulders feel as they hold the worries of your day, all that your eyes have seen and what they might want to tell you about their travels. Playing with this idea of giving voice to parts of our body or voice to what our body does (lungs that breathe, mind that processes, heart that beats and so on) can reveal clues to us about where we are on our journey. The following is a short poem I wrote giving voice to the space my breath creates around my heart.

The space around my heart holds
The words of the women who came before me
The fear of a small child on the first day of school
The hope of a crocus blooming in February
The belief of a traveler who has seen
The truth of a weathered nugget of sea glass

What Contrast Uncovers

Here is another exercise to add to your writer's toolbox: it focuses on using contrast in your writing. The use of opposites and contrast can be helpful because it causes the reader to pause and reflect on what you are conveying with these contrasts. At the same time, coming up with opposites pushes you, the writer, to be specific with your words.

Task: Bring contrast into your writing by finishing the following phrases:

They see . . . I am . . .
The world sees . . . I feel . . .
They expect . . . I wish . . .
They want . . . I want . . .
I am . . . I know . . .

Notes: Come up with your own introductory phrases and finish them. Another idea is to finish beginning phrases like these but then delete the beginning phrases and look at the finished words that remain. Find a poem within those phrases. For example, you might write, "They see . . . someone always there to hold up the world. I am . . . the seed pirouetting to the ground." This might become a poem note that reads something like, "The seed pirouetting to the ground, unable to hold up the world, I seek roots."

Seeing Your Light

This exercise is about celebrating what you see when you look at a photo of yourself.

Task: Look at a photo of yourself (perhaps a self-portrait or a photo someone else has taken of you) and write a poem to or about that photo.

Notes: Consider beginning your poem with a phrase like "I see her/him" as I did in the previous example. Push yourself to look at the words that exist under any negative chatter that comes up. Going back to the example photo on the previous page, the image captures the movement and joy of what dancing is for me. Let yourself get lost in the feeling of your photo to find your words.

Giving Voice to the Body

What is your body telling you? Listening is a practice of mindfulness, enabling you to pause and notice what you might normally ignore.

Task: Choose a part of your body and give that body part a voice.

Notes: Consider beginning your poem with a phrase similar to one of the following:
• My hands show . . .
• Her (His) eyes have seen . . .
• These legs have carried me . . .
• My heart beats the story of . . .

Your poem might be a few lines, or you might find yourself writing several paragraphs. Give yourself permission to listen to what your body has to say.

Focus on the physical: Collage a photo of yourself—in motion—into the frame on the left. It can be, but does not have to be, a photo of you dancing. It could be a photo of you running, singing, cooking . . . anything.

"What Contrast Uncovers": Don't forget to add your own introductory phrases!

They see . . .

I am . . .

The world sees . . .

I feel . . .

They expect . . .

I wish . . .

They want . . .

I want . . .

I am . . .

I know . . .

"Giving Voice to the Body": What might your hands say if they could talk? Your heart? How about your ears?

"Seeing Your Light": Consider using one of the phrases from the "What Contrast Uncovers" exercise, or respond to any negative feeling or words that arise when you look at your photo.

Stream of Consciousness Writing

From *The Journal Junkies Workshop* by Eric M. Scott and David R. Modler

Stream-of-consciousness writing has been a valuable tool for the creative writer for quite a while, and it is just as valuable for the visual journalist. In her book *The Artist's Way*, Julia Cameron discusses what she calls the "morning pages"—three pages she writes in longhand every morning. Julia refers to stream-of-consciousness writing as "brain drain" and explains that this type of writing clears the mind of clutter and makes way for creativity.

Following the lead of fellow visual journalist Jeanne Minnix, we have adapted this concept for use as a timed seven-minute writing exercise on specific topics. The idea is to find a quiet spot, sit for one minute focusing on the topic in silence and then write for seven uninterrupted minutes. The trick is to keep writing. If you find yourself at a point where you cannot think of anything to write, then simply write, "I cannot think of anything to write. I cannot think of anything to write," or write the prompt over and over. Continue this until the writing begins to flow again. Don't worry about spelling, punctuation, grammar or making sense. Just let the writing flow. When time is up, bring your thoughts to a close. You may want to set an audible timer so you don't have to watch the clock.

The more you do this type of writing, the more comfortable you will become with the process. Many times you will find yourself beginning with one topic and winding up writing about something completely different. This could be something that may have been bothering you but that you had not consciously admitted or spoken out loud before. The natural flow of the writing allows things like this to come out. And it is perfectly fine. Stream-of-consciousness writing lets you open up and dump the stuff that gets in the way of your creativity on a page. Writing can be a great spark for a visual journal page as you deal with issues further by adding layers of art.

When we Journal Fodder Junkies do stream-of-consciousness writing, we often make an effort to think about dualistic pairs. These are ideas and concepts that tend to have opposite meanings and associations. We will write on one topic and then a short time later—usually the same day or the next—we will write on the other. In the box, right, are some topics and dualistic pairs to think about.

You can easily come up with your own starter topics simply by writing about a pressing matter. Whatever the topic, it allows you to focus as you write, and some people say having a topic makes stream-of-consciousness writing easier for them.

The question of privacy always comes up due to the nature of stream-of-consciousness writing. Sometimes such writing will take you to a psychological or emotional place that you did not expect to go, and you may write something you wish you had not. We encourage people never to tear pages out of the journal. Instead cover up the writing or obscure it with paint, collage or drawing. It is not important that others read it. It is important that you wrote it, and if it needs to get hidden, that's okay. If it's on a separate piece of paper, you can tear it up and glue it into the journal in a way that makes it impossible to read. Or perhaps you can seal it in an envelope. Some people keep a visual journal strictly for themselves and allow no one to see it. Other people have no problem baring their souls to the world. Find a balance that is comfortable for you.

After you have done some stream-of-consciousness writing, think about various ways that you can incorporate it into your journal. Try writing directly in your journal. Write on other surfaces—tracing paper, vellum, notebook paper or a paper bag—then think about how to put that into your journal. You could collage it, fold it up and put it into an envelope that has been glued in, rip it or cut it up and collage it, or perhaps sew it in. Think about highlighting key words in your writing by making them bold, a different color or rewriting them in larger letters. Also consider stenciling key words and phrases.

Topic:

Set your stopwatch for 8 minutes and GO!

Try These

I believe . . .
I don't believe . . .
I think . . .
I feel . . .
My dream . . .
My nightmare . . .
I want . . .
I need . . .
I love . . .
I hate . . .
I hope . . .
I fear . . .
Light . . .
Dark . . .
Good . . .
Evil . . .
Work . . .
Play . . .

Topic:

Set your stopwatch for 8 minutes and GO!

Now, how do you feel about what you wrote? Is it personal? Too personal? Remember, you can always tear the page out if you feel it necessary, but you can also obscure it in one of so many different ways.

Topic:

Set your stopwatch for 8 minutes and GO!

Think about highlighting key words in your writing by making them bold, a different color or rewriting them in larger letters. Also consider stenciling key words and phrases.

Headlines and Scandals

From *Wide Open* by Randi Feuerhelm-Watts

What do Billy Graham and Jay Leno have in common? They routinely tie current events in with the spoken word. Jokes and Jesus.

If you ever need something to journal about just turn on the news or open a newspaper. Just this morning there was a story about a man in Italy who had slowly been losing his hearing. Then, in one instant, he got his hearing back. While up in a ski lift, he said, something happened and suddenly "pop." What a great jumpstart for a journal page titled, "New Heights for my Journey."

What about the sixteen-year-old prep school student who took a secret, solo trip to Iraq because of his interest in journalism? He even finished writing a paper while he was over there and e-mailed it back to his teacher. There were threats the school was going to expel him, his mom was going to ground him . . . She was quoted as saying, "He always has been very confident." What ever happened to ditching school and going to the movies? Yet there is something quietly heroic about him. Our dreams too often fall flat due to all those reasons why we "shouldn't." These are the stories that make for great writing.

Do you remember listening to the sounds of the crunching, breaking glass as seventy tiles were removed from the collaborative public art piece for the families that lost children in the Columbine shooting? One by one, each tile had to be pried off if it had any reference to God or Jesus. Watching hope crash around their feet reminds us of what pierces our own hearts.

Tape a headline here, or in a couple of sentences, describe the story. Then write. Write about your reaction to it or use it as inspiration.

Poetry

From *Journal Fodder 365* by Eric M. Scott and David R. Modler

You may not consider yourself a poet, but poetry can capture the essence and beauty of a situation or scene. Investigate a variety of forms to tackle a different way of writing, and don't get caught up in the mechanics and rules of the poetry. Allow the verse to flow like water as you tap into your inner depths. Try some of the poetry forms described here, and research some others to give yourself an even wider range of possibilities.

Rhyming Couplets

A rhyming couplet is a set of two lines that end in words that rhyme. This is one of the simplest, most common forms and what many people think of when they hear the term *poetry*. The poem can be a two-line stanza, or you can string together a longer composition from several rhyming couplets. The rhyming scheme can be varied as well to create different rhyming patterns and rhythms.

Haiku

Haiku is a Japanese poetic form that contains just seventeen syllables in three lines. There are five syllables in the first line, seven in the second and five in the third. Although nature is a common subject for haiku, any subject is acceptable. The idea of "cutting," the point where the work is split into two independent yet related ideas or sections, is important. This juxtaposition of ideas brings depth to such a compact poem, allowing the reader to complete the thought of the verse and leaving room for multiple interpretations. Seasonal words are also important in haiku, denoting the time of year. They don't have to be the words spring, fall, October, etc. They can allude to the season, such as baseball, hinting at summer, and snow, suggesting winter.

Free Verse

If the limits and rules of the above forms are a bit too confining and traditional, try free verse. This more contemporary style lacks a predetermined form like haiku or acrostic and uses no rhyme or meter. However, it retains some poetic form and is usually broken into lines, but these lines can vary in length and cadence.

Acrostic

Acrostic is poetry where the first letter of each line spells out a word or phrase, and the subject is often the word spelled out. The lines in acrostic poetry can rhyme, but don't need to. Acrostic easily lends itself to visual representation since the first letter of each line is the emphasis. Embellish and illuminate these letters in a variety of ways to render visual importance. Consider using the name of a person or object as a starter.

Delightfully he pulls people into his sphere,
And shares with them the process of the
Visual journal and all of its possibilities.
Impressed with the potential, these converts
Delve into the depths of their soul.

Eager to connect to the world he
Reaches out through all that he does
Instinctively sharing himself, and
Challenging others to expose their vulnerabilities.

Try it: Rhyming Couplets

Try it: Haiku

Try it: Free Verse

Try it: Acrostic

Keeping a Personal Tally

From *Wide Open* by Randi Feuerhelm-Watts

When I was a little girl we weren't allowed to write out the words *toilet paper* on the grocery list because it was bad manners. We were told to simply put TP. As women, we are list makers. From grocery to birthday to girlfriends who have hurt us, we make lists. Some mentally, some on paper and some we can't find anywhere.

There are lists we would never admit we have—people who should have never done what they did—the "bad" list, the secret "unaccepted" list. We carry these lists in private places we don't talk about. Intertwined with these is the ongoing request list for God. That's the long one.

You can tell a whole story with very few words in the form of a simple list. This form of writing is a great method of adding text to your journal and takes the pressure off the whole sentence structure thing.

A lot of list making goes on in my journal, even if the lists are comprised of things like brightly colored bird eggs and the sound from ringing bells in the university bell tower.

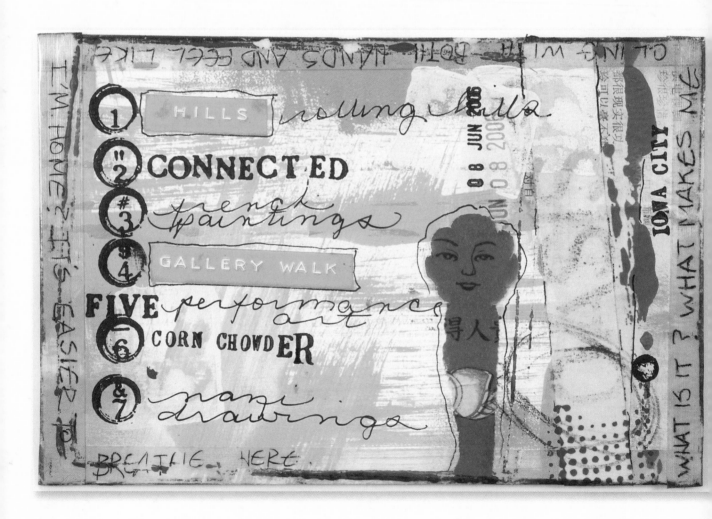

Make a list and check it twice. Let the list speak for itself and tell its own story. Or use one, some or all of the entries as individual prompts later on. Don't forget to embellish the page!

1

2

3

4

5

6

7

8

1 ⎯⎯⎯⎯⎯⎯⎯⎯⎯⎯⎯⎯⎯⎯⎯⎯⎯

2 ⎯⎯⎯⎯⎯⎯⎯⎯⎯⎯⎯⎯⎯⎯⎯⎯⎯

3 ⎯⎯⎯⎯⎯⎯⎯⎯⎯⎯⎯⎯⎯⎯⎯⎯⎯

4 ⎯⎯⎯⎯⎯⎯⎯⎯⎯⎯⎯⎯⎯⎯⎯⎯⎯

5 ⎯⎯⎯⎯⎯⎯⎯⎯⎯⎯⎯⎯⎯⎯⎯⎯⎯

6 ⎯⎯⎯⎯⎯⎯⎯⎯⎯⎯⎯⎯⎯⎯⎯⎯⎯

7 ⎯⎯⎯⎯⎯⎯⎯⎯⎯⎯⎯⎯⎯⎯⎯⎯⎯

8 ⎯⎯⎯⎯⎯⎯⎯⎯⎯⎯⎯⎯⎯⎯⎯⎯⎯

9 ⎯⎯⎯⎯⎯⎯⎯⎯⎯⎯⎯⎯⎯⎯⎯⎯⎯

(1)

(2)

(3)

(4)

(5)

(6)

(7)

What to Journal About

From *Journal Bliss* by Violette

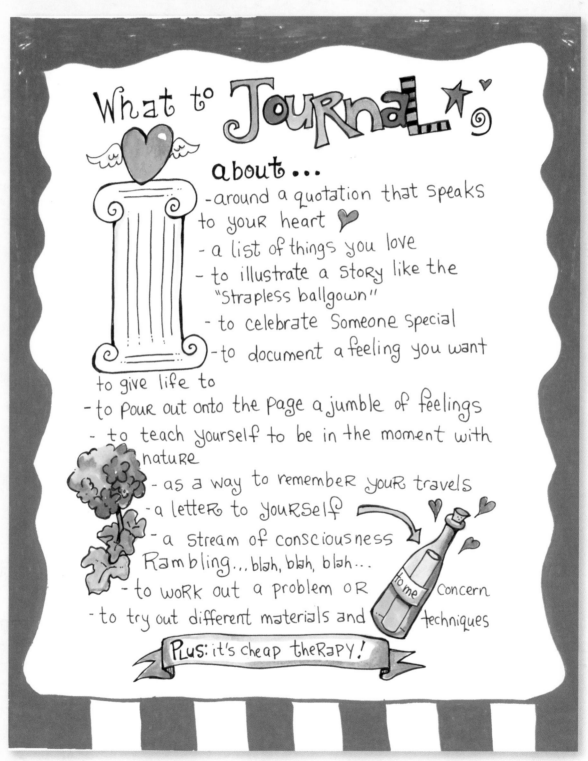

What to JOURNAL...

about...
- around a quotation that speaks to your heart ♥
- a list of things you love
- to illustrate a story like the "Strapless ballgown"
- to celebrate someone special
- to document a feeling you want to give life to
- to pour out onto the page a jumble of feelings
- to teach yourself to be in the moment with nature
- as a way to remember your travels
- a letter to yourself
- a stream of consciousness Rambling...blah, blah, blah...
- to work out a problem or concern
- to try out different materials and techniques

Plus: it's cheap therapy!

Let's start by choosing just one of the prompts on that page over there to the left. Got one? OK, now get writing.

Strategic Planning: Writing Prompts

From *Journal Fodder 365* by Eric M. Scott and David R. Modler

We all have many people we come in contact with on a daily basis; some of those interactions are positive and some are not so positive. As you focus on your writing, keep in mind the wide range of influence others bring into your world. No matter what kind of energy they generate, these relationships affect aspects of our daily decision making. Examine the good, the bad and the ugly, and reflect on how you deal, cope and move forward with these different situations.

These prompts are designed to help you think about your personal journey and your personal mythologies. Writing about each of the prompts allows you to explore the specifics about yourself and inform the decisions you make about the art and images you include in the daily activities.

Writing Prompt 1: Connections, Misconnections and Disconnections

How have you connected and misconnected with people in your life? We seek connections, and many of us have spent an amazing amount of time seeking a spouse, a significant other or a soul mate. We may have found that person or may still be searching, but whether we have found that special link or not, our lives are still filled with family, relatives, friends and co-workers. Sometimes we connect and sometimes we misconnect with these people. What do these connections and misconnections mean to you? How can you deepen the important relationships and disconnect from the not so important ones?

Writing Prompt 2: Inspirations and Nudges

Who inspires you and nudges you? We can't do it all alone, and at times, we need a little nudge to get us going. It is good to have collaborators and accomplices in anything that we do, but especially in our creative endeavors. These people support us, encourage us and, at times, pick us up and carry us when we need them the most. These are our everyday heroes. Who shows up like magic when you need them the most? Who has your back and is always on your side? Who is your hero, your mentor, your collaborator, your accomplice?

Writing Prompt 3: Challengers

Who is challenging you? We all have people in our lives who challenge us. These are people who push and provoke us, who may be downright mean and rude and who don't elicit any warm and fuzzy feelings from us. These are our challengers and at times our arch nemeses. It might be a mother-in-law, a brother, a nosy neighbor, an office bully or our boss. We may even believe these people to be our enemies whose main purpose in life is to torment us, but we can flip our script. Buddhists believe that our enemies are our greatest teachers because they provide us the opportunity to show compassion and understanding and to grow. How can you regard your enemies as your teachers? Why are they challenging to you? What can you learn from these people?

Writing Prompt 4: Inner Connections

How can we connect with others if we don't connect with ourselves? Much of contemporary life seems to be aimed at doing anything and everything so that we are not left alone with our own thoughts. We seem to find a million and one distractions. Perhaps we are afraid of what we will discover if we are alone with our thoughts. Perhaps we are afraid of the self-talk, the never-ending loop of negativity and put-downs. When was the last time you sat in complete silence, alone, and connected with yourself? How do you distract yourself from meaningful dialogue with yourself? How do you find the quiet space to hear your authentic inner voice?

Writing Prompt 5: I Am

Who are you? This seems like a very easy and straight forward question, but when was the last time you really tried to articulate an answer? Take some time to ponder and write about all the aspects of your "self." Think about where you come from, who your family is and what is most important to you. Use adjectives to describe yourself, or describe all of the roles you play or have played in your life. Think about the stories that you build about yourself—the mythology you have constructed.

Writing Prompt 6: Pivotal People

Who in your life has influenced you strongly? This may be in a positive or negative way. Think and write about those people who have had a significant impact in your life and may have been responsible for the direction of your life path. Think about how old you were, how these people affected you, the obstacles that you faced and the way your life has changed. Recognize those who have had a profound effect on you. Who were they? What did they say to you? What do they represent?

Writing Prompt 7: Roads Taken and Not Taken

What have been the important decisions in your life? We have all grown, evolved and changed. At times the movement of our lives has changed direction because of the choices we have made, and at other times it has changed because of the choices that others have made. These are what psychologist Ira Progoff called *Steppingstones* in his Intensive Journal workshop. They are the roads that we have taken and the roads that we have not taken. What have been your stepping stones? What have been the significant moments of change and growth in your life? What have these shifts meant for you and the direction of your life? What have been the opportunities you have pursued—the roads taken? What have been your missed opportunities—the roads not taken?

Writing Prompt 8: Personal Mythologies

What are the stories that you have told yourself over and over again even if they are not true? A myth is a legendary or imaginary narrative that presents our beliefs, and a mythology is a collection of those stories. We have all created myths about ourselves—stories that are imaginary and unverifiable. We have puffed ourselves up with stories of accomplishment and torn ourselves down with stories of lack. We have self-talk, scripts and dialogues running through our heads, reinforcing those myths. Question your own mythology, and see if you can verify the myths. What are your personal myths? What is your personal mythology? What are your stories? Why do you believe them, accept them and perpetuate them?

The "Strategic Planning" writing prompts are terrific prompts for serious, introspective writing. Use them to learn more about yourself and your environment. Which one will you tackle first?

Writing Prompt # ___

Writing Prompt # ___

Writing Prompt # ___

Writing Prompt # ___

4

Visual Journaling

Code Talking
From *Raw Art Journaling* by Quinn McDonald

Remember secret messages written in code? You probably used a code to pass notes in class when you were in grade school. Those same codes and many more can be used just as easily today. A simple replacement code (substitute the letter *A* for the letter *Z*, *B* for *Y* and so on) keeps your secrets and lets you easily untangle them when you are ready. If you like symbols instead of letters, you'll like the frame code. I learned it years ago in Girl Scouts and loved using it as a design around my journal pages. It's easy to learn—you'll be able to use it without studying!

If you have a knack for codes, this one looks exotic and is easy to learn. The solution grid is easy to remember; you could tuck it into a hidden pocket in your journal or write it on one page and glue the facing page to it. To keep the solution usable, glue the edges of the pages with glue dots only. You can easily pry them open, but it's unlikely someone else will look there first.

Materials list

pen you enjoy writing with

your journal

1 Using this grid of letters, replace each letter with the format of lines that surround it on the chart.

2 Indicate that you are using the second letter in a pair by using a dot.

So the words *code* and *secret* would look like this.

This is going to be so much fun! Develop your own code right on this page. Want to keep it a secret? Hide it away in an attached envelope or pocket. If you'd like to use the code keyed on the page to the left, then simply get started writing (although you may wish to hide the key under a flap). What kind of a writing implement will you use? Will you paint the page first? What other type of embellishment will you use?

Continuous Writing

From *Doodles Unleashed* by Traci Bautista

Writing lists and scribbling quotes are fabulous ways to write continuously. Play with different tools as you write to build up layers of color. I use this technique to make creative layers of text that, in the end, look like abstract lines.

Materials list

1 " (2.5cm) foam brush

black, blue and green permanent markers (Sakura Pigma Sensei)

blue ink (Liquitex)

dimensional fabric paint (Tulip Slick)

green and white acrylic paint

highlighter

markers with brush and chisel tips (Copic)

metallic marker (Sakura Permapaque)

Paintastic Brush Pen and Magic Wand (Elmer's)

poster markers

Red Wide marker (Copic)

white correction fluid pen

1 Paint a background with green and white acrylic paint. Dip the brush corners into two different colors and mix the paint on the paper as you brush it onto the surface. Place a little bit of blue ink on a brush and brush it into the wet paint. This will darken areas on the background. Let the paint dry.

2 Write words and phrases using markers of two different colors with brush and chisel tips.

3 Continue writing around the circular-painted design with a metallic marker.

4 Add contrast color with a poster marker and blue and green permanent markers. Scribble more words with a Paintastic Brush Pen and Magic Wand to create variegated colored letters. Write with a highlighter to create transparent letters. The highlighter will blend with the color it is written over.

5 Brighten up the page by writing with a Red Wide marker and a white correction fluid pen over the previous layers. Add contrast with words scribbled in black permanent marker.

6 Add a layer of textured letters by writing with dimensional fabric paint.

Tip} Experiment with creative lettering on fabric. Grab a piece of muslin and a few markers, and make marks and scribbles by writing in layers, switching colors as you work. Paint the fabric with foam or fabric brushes. Create a watercolor effect by loading a little water and paint on the brush.

In the "Continuous Writing" step-by-step, Traci Bautista uses a very specific color palette. Feel free to mimic it. Or shake it up and use whichever colors strike your fancy today. Not only will you be journaling with this technique, you'll also be creating abstract art. Oooh la la.

Journaling on muslin is a fabulous idea, and think of all the possibilities! You could dye the fabric first if you are so inclined. Or better yet, give it a gradated watercolor wash before or after you add your journaling. Collage your fabric journaling into this book—you might want to use a gel medium for this one.

Blobs Are Good

From *Wide Open* by Randi Feuerhelm-Watts

From bright colors, unique borders, layering and creative ways with text, there are endless concepts we can draw from Frida Kahlo's artwork and personal diaries to use in our own journals.

Frida's pages would often have two layers of writing—one on top of the other. (The paler one underneath was impossible to read, but the one in black ink, on the surface was usually legible.) She liked to begin many of her pages by spilling a blob of paint into her book and closing it. This makes for a great intuitive exercise, and one you should try yourself. A few of Frida's pages bled through, but you could put a piece of cardboard behind the pages before spilling the paint to avoid this.

After opening the book, you'll have an abstract blob that you can play around with. Frida would use a crayon and trace around portions of the shape. You can transform the abstract images into self-portraits like she did, or simply pick up whatever is on your work-table, like the bottoms of a paint bottle or a coffee cup. Set it in the paint and make a print of it on the page.

Using a small paintbrush and acrylic paint, write on the background. Don't try to make the letters even. Your handwriting is a reflection of you and says more on a page than a typed or hand-stamped phrase. Make mistakes and work loosely. Doodle around the edges.

Overall, if you find your work is too rigid and contrived, try all of these exercises with your nondominant hand. I promise it works every time.

Paint blob art journaling. Huh. That's a pretty cool idea. Just look at that sample page. There are so many things you can draw from just that. Like hiding writing by spilling paint over it and adding new writing on top of it. Why not try it here?

With this double page, try spilling paint onto one of the pages and then pressing the other page into it for a mirror image. What do you see? This exercise is like looking at the clouds, no? Can you draw into the abstract shapes? Write around the edges? Write in the expansive painted areas?

Free-Floating Bubbles

From *Raw Art Journaling* by Quinn McDonald

Raw art allows your imagination to roam in complete freedom. This design is easy and flexible. No stencils, no templates. Put your hands to paper, and you can be as creative as your day demands.

Materials list
journal

pen you like to doodle with

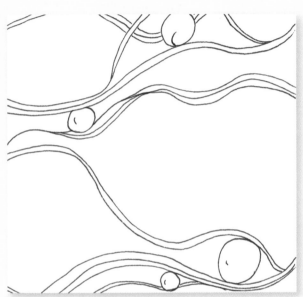

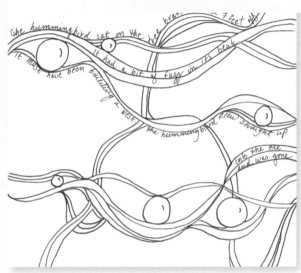

1 Start by drawing a gently curving line across the entire page. Draw another line close to it so it forms a ribbon. Draw freehand without using a template. The unevenness of the lines makes the drawing much more interesting than perfection would. Now draw another line, parallel to the first two. You now have a ribbon with a center stripe. You can see an example of each of these ribbons at the top of the diagram. The thinner ribbon goes under the larger one. In the space between the ribbons, I drew a small circle. The small curved mark on the right side of the circle makes you think of a ball or bubble, and gives the circle another dimension—it's now a sphere.

Continue to draw lines with gentle slopes and waves. Notice that the lines in the ribbon under the space in the middle of the page all connect and then separate. This makes the ribbon look like it is turning.

2 Add as many lines and bubbles as you like—I like to make enough to make the page look interesting but not too busy. Leave some open spaces so you can write. Practice crossing under ribbons, making curves and placing the bubbles so that the lines go behind them.

With raw art, you can stop anytime you want, and then go back days or months later and add more if you want. Raw art is flexible and follows along with your own development and comfort.

In the example, I wrote in the lines because that looked interesting. But don't limit yourself. Write in the spaces you left or even in the bubbles if you make them big enough.

The bubbles are perfect for writing the haiku you wrote earlier in the book. Try writing them in different places until you find a placement that matches your emotions.

There is no "write" or wrong with this one and you are sure to love the results! This is another page ripe for embellishment—maybe with watercolors. What else might you use? What type of writing implement will you use? Quinn suggests a favorite pen, but you could also use colored pencils or markers.

Resources

Art Supplies

Arizona Art Supply
arizonaartsupply.com

Artist Cellar
artistcellar.com

Changing Hands Bookstore
changinghands.com

Character Constructions
characterconstructions.com

Coffee Break Design
coffeebreakdesign.com

Collage Closet
collagecloset.com

The Craft Retreat
thecraftretreat.com

The Crafter's Workshop
thecraftersworkshop.com

Crayola
crayola.com

Daniel Smith
danielsmith.com

Golden Artist Colors
goldenpaints.com

Grafix Plastics
grafixplastics.com

Hollander's
hollanders.com

John Neal Bookseller
johnnealbooks.com

June Tailor
junetailor.com

M. Graham
mgraham.com

Moleskine
moleskine.com

New York Central Art Supply
nycentralart.com

Pilot
pilotpen.com

Ranger Ink & Innovative Craft Products
rangerink.com

SkyBluePink
skybluepink.com

Strathmore
strathmoreartist.com

Teesha Moore Techniques
teeshamoore.com

Tsukineko
tsukineko.com

Volcano Arts
volcanoarts.com

Winsor & Newton
winsornewton.com

Books

Andreas, Brian. *Mostly True*. Decorah, IA: Storypeople Press, 2008

Arrien, Angeles. *Signs of Life: The Five Universal Shapes and How to Use Them*. New York: Jeremy P. Tarcher/Putnam, 1998.

Beam, Mary Todd. *Celebrate Your Creative Self: More than 25 Exercises to Unleash the Artist Within*. Cincinnati, OH: North Light Books, 2001.

Cameron, Julia. *The Artist's Way: A Spiritual Path to Higher Creativity*. New York: Jeremy P. Tarcher/Putnam, 1992.

Carter, David A., and James Diaz. *Elements of Pop-Up: A Pop-Up Book for Aspiring Paper Engineers*. New York: Little Simon, 1999.

Chopin, Kate. *The Awakening*.

Diehn, Gwen. *Real Life Journals: Designing and Using Homemade Books*. Asheville, NC: Lark Crafts, 2010.

Diehn, Gwen. *The Decorated Page: Journals, Scrapbooks & Albums Made Simply Beautiful*. New York: Lark Books, 2002.

Dobie, Jeanne. *Making Color Sing: Practical Lessons in Color and Design*. New York: Watson Guptill, 1986.

Edwards, Betty. *Drawing on the Right Side of the Brain*. Los Angeles: Jeremy P. Tarcher/Putnam, 1989.

Eldon, Kathy. *The Journey Is the Destination: The Journals of Dan Eldon*. San Francisco: Chronicle Books, 1997.

Goldberg, Natalie. *Long Quiet Highway*. New York: Bantam, 1994

Harrison, Sabrina Ward. *Brave on the Rocks: If You Don't Go, You Don't See*. New York: Villiard Books, 2001.

Harrison, Sabrina Ward. *Messy Thrilling Life: The Art of Figuring Out How to Live*. New York: Villiard Books, 2004.

Harrison, Sabrina Ward. *Spilling Open: The Art of Becoming Yourself*. New York: Villiard Books, 1999.

Jennings, Simon. *The New Artist's Manual*. San Francisco: Chronicle Books, 2005.

Kahlo, Frida. *The Diary of Frida Kahlo: An Intimate Self-Portrait*. New York: Harry N. Abrams, 1995.

Kaupelis, Robert. *Experimental Drawing*. New York: Watson-Guptill, 1980.

LaPlantz, Shereen. *Cover to Cover: Creative Techniques for Making Beautiful Books, Journals and Albums*. New York: Sterling Publishing, 1995.

LeLand, Nita. *The Creative Artist: A Fine Artist's Guide to Expanding Your Creativity and Achieving Your Artistic Potential*. Cincinnati, OH: North Light Books, 1990.

New, Jennifer. *Dan Eldon: The Art of Life*. San Francisco: Chronicle Books, 2001.

New Jennifer. *Drawing from Life: The Journal as Art*. New York: Princeton Architectural Press, 2005.

Perrella, Lynne. *Artist's Journals and Sketchbooks: Exploring and Creating Personal Pages*. Gloucester, MA: Quarry Books, 2004.

SARK. *Succulent Wild Woman*. New York: Touchstone, 1997

Sonheim, Carla. *Drawing Lab for Mixed Media Artists*. Minneapolis, MN: Quarry Books, 2010.

Steinhart, Peter. *The Undressed Art: Why We Draw*. New York: Vintage Books, 2005.

Zollner, Frank. *Leonardo da Vinci: Complete Paintings and Drawings*. Los Angeles: Taschen, 2003.

About the Authors

Collage Unleashed

Traci Bautista is a mixed-media artist, designer and author of the best-selling books *Collage Unleashed* and *Doodles Unleashed*. Her art has been featured in over fifty art and mixed-media publications, numerous blogs, and HGTV and DIY networks. She designs licensed product lines, Collage Pauge adhesive and {kolLAJ} papercrafts. Follow her musings at treicdesigns.com or at her blog, creativityUN-LEASHED, at kollaj.typepad.com.

Wide Open

Randi Feuerhelm-Watts is the author of *Wide Open: Inspiration and Techniques for Art Journaling on the Edge*.

Inner Excavation

Liz Lamoreux has found herself drawn to the stories told by images from her childhood—vintage handkerchiefs, bowls of seashells, glass bottles and her grandmother's sewing basket. She believes that unearthing our stories and sharing them through creating, writing and community are vital to connecting with the journey that is life. She lives with her husband, daughter and their golden retriever, Millie, in a small house just the right size for their little family, in the beautiful Pacific Northwest, where she can often be found in her studio surrounded by strips of fabric, vintage buttons, several idea and poetry journals and a mug of tea. As a yoga teacher and artist, she sees creating as a meditative exercise for the spirit and is currently focusing on sharing this inward journey with others. Find out more about her adventures at lizlamoreux.com.

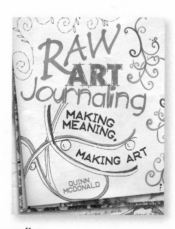

Raw Art Journaling

Quinn McDonald is a certified creativity coach who creates art, writes, teaches and rides her motorcyle in the amazing landscape of the Sonoran desert with her husband, Kent. Her son, Ian, is a professor of music theory at Yale University. Quinn is grateful that she inherited her father's wry sense of humor and her mother's ability to make incredible gravy from scratch. You can find Quinn at her blog Quinncreative.wordpress.com or website Quinncreative.com. You can also find her on Facebook, Twitter, Pinterest and Flickr.

The Journal Junkies Workshop and *Journal Fodder 365*

David R. Modler is an artist/educator born and raised in Baltimore. He earned his Bachelor of Science and Master of Education in art education from Towson State University and taught elementary art for fifteen years. David earned his Master of Fine Arts in drawing and painting from James Madison University in Harrisonburg, Virginia, and now holds a teaching position at Appalachian State University in Boone, North Carolina.

Eric M. Scott is an artist/educator born and raised in Washington, Pennsylvania. Earning his Bachelor of Science in art education from Edinboro University of Pennsylvania, he currently lives in Purcellville, VA. Eric is a National Board Certified teacher and teaches art for Loudoun County Public Schools.

In 2005, David and Eric teamed up to officially become the Journal Fodder Junkies (JFJ), and they have been spreading the power and the joy of the visual journal to all who seek creative release. David and Eric have continued to provide workshops, presentations, and seminars to teachers, students and artists throughout the country, and they have co-authored the best-selling books, *The Journal Junkies Workshop: Visual Ammunition for the Art Addict* and *Journal Fodder 365: Daily Doses of Inspiration for the Art Addict*.

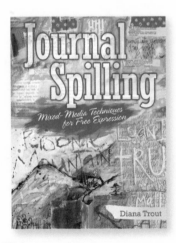

Journal Spilling

Diana Trout is a painter, book artist and teacher. She studied painting at the University of the Arts and Pennsylvania Academy of the Fine Arts in Philadelphia. She has shown her work at craft shows and galleries in the Philadelphia area, New York and New Jersey. Diana has taught classes and workshops in painting, journaling, general art and book arts and has taught origami to children and adults at art centers, libraries, national venues and from her studio. Diana has two kids and lives in the little town of Glenside with her husband, cat and a bunch of birds and squirrels. Contact her at: dianatrout.com.

Journal Bliss

Violette is a creative spirit who lives in a purple magic cottage with Mr. G—aptly named for his tolerance of glitter found in food, clothing and some of the strangest places. Violette's art has been featured in books, magazines, newspapers and television worldwide. She follows her bliss by inspiring others to embrace who they are by teaching workshops on visual journaling and collage. Violette can be spotted near the quaint seaside community of White Rock, British Columbia. You can visit her blog at violette.ca or her website, purplejuice.ca.

Index

a
acrostics, 85, 89

b
Bautista, Traci, 32, 108, 110, 124
body, listening to, 66–69, 71
books
  altered, 25
  as resource, 122–123
box, of words, 58–63
bubbles, free-floating, 118–119

c
Cameron, Julia, 74
Carson, Richard, 13
codes, 104–105
color spilling, 19, 116
contrast, 67, 70
crayons, 26
crossword puzzles, 46, 48

d
doodling, 32–35,114
duct tape, 46

e
electrical tape, 46
embellishment, 85, 91
envelopes, 105
ephemera, 52

f
fabric, lettering on, 109, 112
Feuerhelm-Watts, Randi, 5, 46, 80, 90, 114, 124
free verse, 85, 88

g
gesso, 5, 19–20, 54
graphite pencils, 25
gremlin. See also inner critic

dealing with, 6–11
silencing, 12–15

h
haiku, 84, 87, 118
headlines, 80–81
highlighting, 74, 79

i
inks, 47, 108
inner critic. See also gremlin
  dealing with, 6–11
  identifying, 21–22
  silencing, 12–15
  taming, 18–23
inner poet, 66–67, 84–85
  See also poetry

j
journal spilling, 18–19
journal writing, daily, 52–54
journaling, 5
  subjects for, 94
journals, visual, 52, 74

k
Kahlo, Frida, 114

l
Lamoreux, Liz, 5, 66, 124
layering, 74, 108
lettering, fanciful, 40–42
list-making, 90–94, 108
lyrics, 25, 28–29

m
markers, 26, 108–109
McDonald, Quinn, 5–6, 58, 60, 104, 118–119, 124
medical tape, 47
Modler, David R., 52, 74, 84, 98, 125
muslin, writing on, 109, 112
mythologies, personal, 99

n
newspaper clippings, 46, 48, 80–81
note taking, 25

o
origami box, 58

p
packing tape, 46
paint
  acrylic, 46, 54, 109, 114
  blobs, 114–115
  spilling, 19, 116
  watercolor, 48
pencils, 25–26
pens, 26
photographs, 66, 68–69, 73
pockets, 105
poetry, 25, 84–89. See also inner poet
printed text, 24
prompts, for writing, 60–63, 98–103

q
quotes, 25, 94, 108

r
raw art, 118
resources, 122–123
rhyming couplets, 84, 86

s
Scott, Eric M., 52, 74, 84, 98, 125
scribbling, 109
self-awareness, 68–69, 71, 73, 99
self-portrait, 18–23, 114
stamps, 24, 27, 46
stencils, 24, 27, 46, 74, 79
stream of consciousness, 74–79, 94

supplies, 3
  sources for, 122
surfaces, for writing, 74

t
tape, 46–47
text. See also words
  drawn, 24, 27
  experimenting with, 24–29
  fanciful lettering, 40–42
  found, 24
  layering, 108–109
  printed, 24
tools, experimenting with, 24–27, 30, 94
Trochelman, Lynn, 7
Trout, Diana, 18, 125

v
Violette, 12 , 40, 94, 125

w
washi tape, 47
watercolor crayons, 26
watercolor pencils, 26
watercolor spill, 19
watercolor washes, 48, 112
whiteout pen, 33
words. See also text
  in a box, 58–63
writing
  continuous, 108–110
  in code, 104–105
  prompts for, 60–63, 98–103
  spill writing, 19
  stream of consciousness, 74–79, 94
writing implements, 25–27, 30, 40

Other fine North Light Books are available from your favorite bookstore, art supply store or online supplier. Visit our website at fwmedia.com.

17 16 15 14 13   5 4 3 2 1

DISTRIBUTED IN CANADA BY FRASER DIRECT
100 Armstrong Avenue
Georgetown, ON, Canada L7G 5S4
Tel: (905) 877-4411

DISTRIBUTED IN THE U.K. AND EUROPE
BY F&W MEDIA INTERNATIONAL, LTD
Brunel House, Forde Close, Newton Abbot,
TQ12 4PU, UK
Tel: (+44) 1626 323200, Fax: (+44) 1626 323319
Email: enquiries@fwmedia.com

DISTRIBUTED IN AUSTRALIA BY CAPRICORN LINK
P.O. Box 704, S. Windsor NSW, 2756 Australia
Tel: (02) 4560 1600, Fax: (02) 4577 5288
Email: books@capricornlink.com.au

ISBN-13: 978-1-4403-2907-4

Edited by Amy Jones
Designed by Geoff Raker
Production coordinated by Greg Nock

fwmedia.com

Metric Conversion Chart

To convert	to	multiply by
Inches	Centimeters	2.54
Centimeters	Inches	0.4
Feet	Centimeters	30.5
Centimeters	Feet	0.03
Yards	Meters	0.9
Meters	Yards	1.1

The Whole Story. Your Story.

Want more ideas for making and sharing your story? Scan the QR code with your smartphone's QR code reader or visit CreateMixedMedia.com/mixed-media-storytelling for more.

These and other fine North Light mixed-media products are available at your local art & craft retailer, bookstore or online supplier. Visit our website at CreateMixedMedia.com

Find the latest issues of *Cloth Paper Scissors* magazine on newsstands, or visit shop.clothpaperscissors.com!

CreateMixedMedia.com

- Connect with your favorite mixed-media artists.
- Get the latest in mixed-media inspiration, tips and techniques.
- Be the first to get special deals on the products you need to improve your mixed-media art.

 Follow *CreateMixedMedia* for the latest news, free wallpapers, free demos and chances to win FREE BOOKS!

 Follow us! @cMixedMedia

 Follow us! *CreateMixedMedia*

For inspiration delivered to your inbox, sign up for our FREE e-mail newsletter.